CHAPTERS IN HISTORY

W9-BVL-032

Who Cracked the Liberty Bell?
And Other Questions About the American Revolution

by Peter and Connie Roop

SCHOLASTIC INC.
New York Toronto London Auckland Sydney
Mexico City New Delhi Hong Kong Buenos Aires

For Faye and her family—
Thanks for the years of friendship and fellowship!
—C. R. and P. R.

ISBN-13: 978-0-439-02523-2
ISBN-10: 0-439-02523-0

Text copyright © 2007 by Peter and Connie Roop
Illustrations copyright © 2007 by Scholastic Inc.

All rights reserved. Published by Scholastic Inc.

SCHOLASTIC and associated logos are trademarks and/or registered trademarks of Scholastic Inc.

12 11 10 9 8 7 6   11 12/0

Printed in the U.S.A.
First printing, November 2007

Contents

CHAPTER 1

What Is Patriots' Day?

Every year in April, the people in Massachusetts celebrate Patriots' Day. There are parades, races, fireworks, and fun. Why does Massachusetts celebrate Patriots' Day? They celebrate because the American Patriots began their fight for freedom in Massachusetts on April 19, 1775.

The Revolutionary War Begins

British soldiers in Boston had orders to march out of the city. They wanted to capture John Hancock and Sam Adams. These two Patriot leaders were staying outside of Boston in Lexington, Massachusetts. They also wanted to take the cannons and gunpowder the

Patriots had stored in nearby Concord. The British planned to march out of Boston early on April 19, 1775.

The Patriots Are Warned

American Patriots in Boston learned the British plans. Paul Revere, a Patriot, rode through the countryside shouting that the British soldiers were

Fact

Paul Revere was captured by the British, but he escaped.

coming out of Boston. Other riders shouted warnings, too. American Patriots grabbed their guns. Some went to Lexington. Others went to Concord.

The Battle of Lexington

Dozens of American Patriots lined up against the British in Lexington. Suddenly, someone fired a gun. No one knows who fired first. Maybe it was a British soldier. Maybe a Patriot fired first. When the firing stopped, eight Patriots had been killed. Only one British soldier died. The British had won the first battle of the Revolutionary War!

Fact

Lexington is about fifteen miles west of Boston.

The Battle of Concord

The British soldiers marched to Concord. Four hundred Patriots waited for the British at North Bridge. The British fired first. The Patriots fired back. The battle lasted two hours before the British gave up. They marched back to Boston. The Patriots had won the second battle of the Revolutionary War!

The Battle Road

The Patriots followed the British on the road back to Boston. The Patriots fired at the

British from behind trees, walls, fences, rocks, barns, and houses. Over three hundred British soldiers died before the British army was back in Boston. The British stayed in Boston until they could safely sail away the next year.

First Shots

The Revolutionary War began on April 19, 1775. American Patriots and British soldiers fired the first shots of the Revolutionary War that morning. In 1781, the Revolutionary War ended when the American Patriots defeated the British. Patriots' Day celebrates this important chapter in history. Do you think all Americans should celebrate on April 19?

Fact

Patriots were called "Minutemen" because they had to be ready to fight in a minute.

CHAPTER 2

Who Was Invited to the Boston Tea Party?

No one sent invitations to the Boston Tea Party. It wasn't really a party at all! The British and Americans were fighting about the price of tea. Americans felt that the British were charging too much money for tea from England. They wanted to teach the British a lesson, so one night they dumped a lot of tea into the ocean. This event was called the Boston Tea Party.

Tax Time

The British government wanted money from the American colonies. The government charged extra money for things like tea, cloth,

glass, paper, and paint. This extra money was
called a tax. The Americans did not think the
taxes were fair. They did not want to pay the
taxes. The British government did not take
away the taxes, so the Americans came up
with a plan.

Boycott

The angry Americans decided to stop
buying products from Britain. This is called
a boycott. Americans made their own cloth.

They made their own tea out of roots. They made their own glass and paint.

The Boycott Ends

Americans did not buy British goods. British shopkeepers lost lots of money. The shopkeepers asked their government to end the taxes. The government listened to the shopkeepers. They ended the taxes on everything but tea. The Americans ended their boycott. They bought everything but tea.

Tea Comes to Boston

In December, 1773 three ships loaded with tea sailed into Boston Harbor. The people of Boston were told to pay the tax on the tea. But no one would pay the tea tax. Instead, the people of Boston called a big meeting to talk about the tea. Five thousand people came to the meeting! Instead of paying the tea tax, they decided to dump the tea into the harbor.

The Boston Tea Party

On the night of December 16, 1773, fifty men and boys dressed up like Native Americans. They silently climbed aboard the tea ships. They split open the tea chests. They spilled the tea into the sea. That

night, they dumped three hundred and forty-two chests of tea into the harbor.

An Unhappy King

King George was very angry about the Boston Tea Party. He sent his army to Boston. He would not let any ships come to Boston to bring the food and supplies that the Americans needed. But the rest of the colonies came to Boston's rescue. They sent sheep, cows, and other supplies to Boston.

After the Tea Party

After the Boston Tea Party feelings between America and Britain grew worse. The Boston Tea Party made the Americans realize that they wanted freedom from Britain. A year and a half after the Boston Tea Party, the Revolutionary War began. America won the war and became free because of tea!

CHAPTER 3

Who Was Yankee Doodle and Why Do We Sing About Him?

Yankee Doodle went to town,
Riding on a pony,
Stuck a feather in his hat,
And called it macaroni.

Americans have been singing about Yankee Doodle since the Revolutionary War. Today, *Yankee Doodle* is one of America's favorite songs.

Who Was Yankee Doodle?

There was no real person named Yankee Doodle. He was made up by British soldiers to tease American patriots.

"Yankee" meant an American. This is what the British soldiers called the people of New England. A "doodle" was someone who acted like a fool. To the British, a "Yankee Doodle" was an American fool.

Yankee Doodle Music

The tune for *Yankee Doodle* was hummed and played long before the Revolutionary War began. The music for *Yankee Doodle* came from an old English tune. The tune was simple and

easy to remember. It was easy to play on a fife and drum.

Macaroni in a Hat?

Yankees did put feathers on their hats. But they did not call them "macaroni." Yankees liked to decorate their hats with feathers, raccoon tails, and pieces of evergreen.  The British soldiers put "macaroni" in their Yankee Doodle song to make fun of the way the Americans dressed.

American Victory Song

The British soldiers did not think that an army of "Yankee Doodles" could fight against them.

The American soldiers surprised the British. They fought hard. They fought bravely. They won battles. The British stopped singing *Yankee Doodle*.

American patriots, however, began singing *Yankee Doodle* proudly. *Yankee Doodle* became a victory song for the American soldiers.

> *Yankee Doodle is the tune,*
> *That we all delight in:*
> *It suits for feasts, it suits for fun,*
> *And just as well for fighting!*

George Washington's Verse

Yankee Doodle became a favorite American song. All through the Revolutionary War, American soldiers made up new verses to *Yankee Doodle*. They sang this verse about George Washington:

> *There was Captain Washington,*
> *Upon a slapping stallion...*

A-givin' orders to his men,
I guess there was a million.

Popular Song

Today, *Yankee Doodle* is one of America's most popular songs. We sing *Yankee Doodle* in concerts. We play *Yankee Doodle* on musical instruments. There never was a real "Yankee Doodle," but Americans still proudly *mind the music and the step* and sing about our Yankee Doodle Dandy.

Activity

Can you make up your own verse?

CHAPTER 4

Why Is the Fourth of July Called Independence Day?

Every Fourth of July we wear red, white, and blue, and celebrate with picnics and fireworks. But do you know why this day is so important to Americans? During the

Revolutionary War, American Patriots were fighting against British soldiers for freedom. The American Congress was working hard to find a way to tell the British government that it wanted to be independent. On July 4, 1776, the Declaration of Independence was signed.

Thomas Jefferson's Job

Congress asked five men to write the Declaration of Independence. They were Thomas Jefferson, Benjamin Franklin, John Adams, Roger Sherman, and Robert Livingston. Thomas Jefferson was asked to write the first draft. Jefferson needed to use powerful words to tell the world that America had declared its independence from Britain.

Fact

Thomas Jefferson was the youngest man on the committee.

Writing the Declaration

Jefferson put four important ideas in the Declaration of Independence. He told the world why the colonies wanted to be free. He said what King George had done wrong to

Fact

Jefferson wrote for seventeen days!

Americans. He explained what Americans thought a good government should be. And he stated that all men were created equal. Only a few small changes were made to Thomas Jefferson's famous words.

Congress Votes

On June 28, 1776, the Declaration of Independence was read out loud to Congress. Congress agreed with Jefferson's words. Five days later, on July 2, 1776, Congress voted to declare independence.

Independence Day

On July 4, John Hancock, the President of Congress, signed the Declaration of Independence. He signed his name in big, bold,

Fact

Today, the phrase, "Signing your John Hancock" means writing your signature.

black letters. Hancock said he wrote his name large so that the King of England could read it without his glasses! From that day on, July 4 has been known as Independence Day.

Independence!

Copies of the Declaration of Independence were printed quickly. Riders carried the Declaration from Philadelphia to the other colonies. On July 9, 1776, the Declaration was read to General Washington's cheering soldiers in New York. The Declaration was read in town halls, inns, and outdoor meeting places. Cannons boomed, guns fired, fireworks exploded, and statues of King George were pulled down. Everywhere Patriots yelled "Huzzah! Huzzah! Huzzah!" for independence. Patriots throughout the colonies fought even harder to win the Revolutionary War. And they did! So the next time you celebrate the Fourth of July, think about all that you are celebrating!

CHAPTER 5

Who Cracked the Liberty Bell?

The big zigzag crack in the Liberty Bell is easy to see. But who cracked the Liberty Bell? No one knows. This is one chapter in history we will always wonder about.

A New Bell

In 1751, the people of Philadelphia, Pennsylvania, wanted a new bell. They wanted to ring the bell to announce good news and bad news. The new bell would hang in the Pennsylvania State House.

Made in England

The best bellmakers were in England. The people of Philadelphia wanted a bell that weighed 2,000 pounds. They wanted the words "Proclaim Liberty thro' all the Land" on their new bell.

Something Is Wrong!

In August, 1753, the new bell arrived from England. The bell was beautiful. People in Philadelphia were proud. They couldn't wait to hear their new bell ring.

A bell ringer pulled the rope that made the bell sound.

Bong! Bong! Boooooong! rang the new bell.

But something was wrong! The bell sounded strange. The new bell had cracked!

Another New Bell

The people of Philadelphia decided to make a new bell out of the cracked bell.

Two American bellmakers named John Pass and John Stow broke the bell into pieces. They melted the pieces. They made a new bell.

Pass and Stow put their names on the new bell.

Ringing for Independence

On July 8, 1776, people heard the bell ringing loudly. The bell was calling them to hear the Declaration of Independence being read for the first time. The bell was named the Independence Bell.

Fact

During the Revolutionary War, the Liberty Bell was hidden to keep the British from melting it down to make cannons.

Fact

This bell wasn't called the Liberty Bell until 1839.

The Liberty Bell Cracks Again!

The Liberty Bell was rung many times over the years. The bell rang on the Fourth of July to celebrate the birthday of the United States.

The bell rang when Benjamin Franklin died.

On February 22, 1846, the Liberty Bell rang to celebrate the anniversary of George Washington's birthday.

Bong! Bong! Bong! The bell rang loud and clear.

Boooong! Suddenly, a big crack zigzagged from the middle to the bottom of the bell.

Fact

The crack is a ½ inch wide and 2 feet long.

The Liberty Bell had cracked again!

World's Most Famous Bell

The Liberty Bell is the most famous bell in the world. Each year millions of visitors from around the world come to see the Liberty Bell in Philadelphia. But no one will hear the cracked Liberty Bell ring again. Don't you wish you could hear the Liberty Bell ring?

CHAPTER 6

Did Children Spy for George Washington?

General George Washington needed many spies to help him win the Revolutionary War. But were any of those spies children?

Yes! A girl spy saved George Washington's life. A boy spy carried secret messages inside his coat buttons. Another girl rode thirty miles to let American soldiers know the British were coming to attack them. A boy sewed secret letters into his coat. Many other children helped George Washington and his army win the Revolutionary War.

Spies Are Important

George Washington knew how important spies could be. Spies found out when British armies planned to attack. They learned where the British armies kept their supplies. They discovered British plots to steal General Washington's secrets.

Most of General Washington's spies were adults, but many children also helped.

Phoebe Fraunces

Fourteen-year-old Phoebe Fraunces helped her father run his inn in New York City. The inn was George Washington's favorite place to eat.

One day Phoebe spied on a British solider. She heard that he was planning to kill George Washington by putting green poison on his peas at dinner. Phoebe grabbed General Washington's plate of poisoned peas. She threw them out the window to some chickens. The chickens died, but Phoebe had saved George Washington's life!

John Darragh

In 1777, General Washington wanted to know when the British were going to attack his army. Lydia Darragh, an American spy, learned the British plans.

Lydia wrote the British plans on pieces of paper, which she then hid inside her son John's coat buttons. John would carry the messages to General Washington. This was very dangerous. If the British found the secret messages they might capture John as a spy.

John safely reached General Washington. Thanks to the messages inside John's buttons, the American army was ready for the British attack.

Mary Redmond

When Mary Redmond was about twelve years old, she was part of a spy team. A boy (we don't know his name) brought secret letters to Mary. He carried the letters hidden inside the back of his coat.

One day, British soldiers stopped Mary's spy partner. Mary knew that they might find the hidden letter so she playfully tackled her friend. While they wrestled on the ground, Mary slipped the letter out of her partner's coat. She hid the letter in her dress. Then Mary skipped away with the secret letter.

Beulah and Susannah Murray

General Howe's British army was chasing George Washington's army. General Howe stopped at Mary Murray's house to rest.

Mary Murray planned to trick General Howe so he could not catch the American army. She told her young daughters, Beulah and Susannah, her plan. Then Mary invited General Howe to stay for lunch.

General Howe enjoyed the delicious meal. While he ate, Beulah and Susannah told stories and sang songs.

The British soldiers stayed so long enjoying the food and entertainment that the American army had time to escape.

Help for George Washington

American Patriots helped General Washington in many different ways. Some were soldiers. Some were sailors. Some made guns. And some, including children, were spies. Do you think you could have been a spy for General Washington?

Fact

Spies often wrote their secrets in invisible ink.

CHAPTER 7

Did Betsy Ross Really Sew the First Flag of the United States?

Betsy Ross sewed many flags. She sewed British flags before the Revolutionary War. She sewed American flags during the war. She sewed more American flags after the war ended. But did Betsy Ross really sew the first flag of the United States? The answer is ...maybe!

Sewing Skills

Betsy grew up in Philadelphia. She had many brothers and sisters. Betsy helped her

mother cook, clean, and mend clothes. She especially enjoyed sewing. Betsy sewed skirts for her sisters and shirts for her brothers. Betsy even won a contest in school for her sewing skills.

Shop Years

When she was twelve years old, Betsy began sewing in a shop. The shop sold blankets, curtains, tablecloths, and flags. John

Ross also worked there. Betsy and John were married in 1773, and they opened their own shop. Betsy and John lived upstairs above the shop. Their business was very successful.

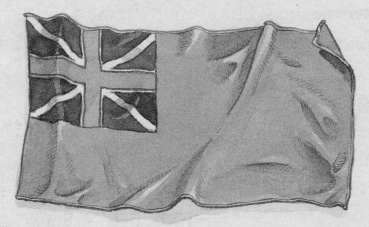

Revolutionary War Begins

In 1776, the Revolutionary War was being fought against England. Betsy and John were American Patriots. While Betsy worked in their shop, John served as a soldier. John's job was to guard the gunpowder for General Washington. One day, the gunpowder accidentally exploded. Sadly, John Ross was killed.

Shop Stays Open

After John died, Betsy kept their shop open. She stayed busy making and selling things. Betsy made clothes for officers in the American army. She even made shirts for General George Washington!

Flag Story

A famous story ties Betsy Ross to the first American flag.

One day, George Washington and two men came to Betsy's shop. They wanted Betsy to make a flag for the United States. They wanted the flag to have six white stripes and seven red stripes. They also wanted thirteen white stars on a blue background.

Fact

The stars and stripes stood for the thirteen American states.

George Washington thought the stars should have six points. Betsy quickly folded a piece of paper. *Snip, snip, snip* went her scissors as she cut out a star. Betsy's star only had five points. General Washington liked Betsy's star with five points.

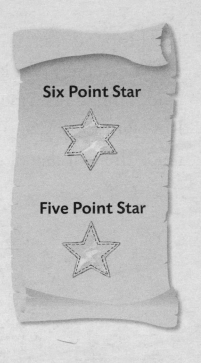

Six Point Star

Five Point Star

Betsy Ross wasn't the only person asked to make an American flag. But, Betsy's was picked to be the first flag of the United States. Or so the story goes!

American Flagmaker

History does not tell us for sure that Betsy Ross made the very first American flag.

But history does tell us that she made many American flags. We know Betsy Ross was paid for making American flags during the Revolutionary War. Do you think Betsy Ross made the first flag of the United States?

CHAPTER 8

Why Is the Bald Eagle Our National Symbol?

The bald eagle is the national symbol of the United States. This bird stands for strength and freedom. But who chose the bald eagle to be our national symbol? And why was the bald eagle picked instead of another animal? The answers are an interesting chapter in our history.

The Seal of the United States

On July 4, 1776, the American Congress was busy. It declared independence from Britain, and the United States was born. That same day, Congress asked a committee to make

a seal, or stamp, for the new nation. The seal would be stamped on important government papers.

Seal Design

Congress wanted the seal to represent the thirteen states of the United States. They wanted the seal to stand for the strength of the new nation. They wanted the seal to show that the United States was also a peaceful country.

Choosing an Animal

Congress wanted an animal to stand for the United States. But what animal could stand for America? One person suggested a dove; another wanted a rooster. Ben Franklin suggested the rattlesnake because of its deadly fangs. A rattlesnake's thirteen rattles also reminded Ben of the thirteen states. Ben also suggested that a turkey be selected for the seal.

The Bald Eagle Is Chosen

Finally, the bald eagle was chosen to

Fact

Bald eagles are not really bald. They look bald because of the white feathers on their heads.

stand as the symbol of the United States.

Congress chose the bald eagle because it is strong and free, and is found only in North America. The bald eagle on the Great Seal holds important symbols in its strong claws. It holds an olive branch in its right claw. The olive branch stands for peace. The eagle also holds thirteen arrows in its left claw. The arrows stand for war. There are thirteen arrows, one for each of the first thirteen states.

America Wins the War

Congress knew that the seal would not really be needed until the United States won

the Revolutionary War. In 1781, at Yorktown, Virginia, General Washington defeated the British. The United States had won the war!

On June 20, 1782, Congress approved the Great Seal of the United States.

A Turkey?

In 1784, Ben Franklin wrote a letter to his daughter Sally. He said he wished that the bald eagle had not been chosen. Ben felt that the turkey had more courage than an eagle. Ben wrote that the turkey was a "true, original native of America." But in 1782, Ben used the bald eagle seal on his official papers.

The Eagle Soars

Today, thousands of bald eagles soar in our skies. Bald eagles decorate our schools. Sports teams are named Eagles. The next time you have a dollar bill, look on the back. Can you find the bald eagle, the symbol of the United States?